To Nic

The Weather House

Thanks for a lovely evening,

Susan Taylor
Susan
&
Simon Williams
Simon

Indigo Dreams Publishing

First Edition: The Weather House
First published in Great Britain in 2017 by:
Indigo Dreams Publishing
24, Forest Houses
Cookworthy Moor
Halwill
Beaworthy
Devon
EX21 5UU

www.indigodreams.co.uk

ISBN 978-1-910834-62-6
British Library Cataloguing in Publication Data. A CIP record for this book can be obtained from the British Library.

Designed and typeset in Palatino Linotype by Indigo Dreams.
Cover design by Simon Williams and Ronnie Goodyer from artwork by Hannah Kopacz.
Printed and bound in Great Britain by 4edge Ltd.

Papers used by Indigo Dreams are recyclable products made from wood grown in sustainable forests following the guidance of the Forest Stewardship Council.

Susan Taylor

Acknowledgements

Spring Bank Holiday was first published in *Lincoln Green*. *Yin Yang* and *Deli Morning* appeared first in *This Given*, Paper Dart Press. *Out of Hibernation* was included in *Moor Poets II* and *And Again* was published in *Love & Ensuing Madness*, www.ratassreview.net.

Previous publications

Unbroken – Poetry Nottingham Pamphlets
Lincoln Green – Lincolnshire and Humberside Arts
The Complete Bearded Stranger – Taxvs Press
Rose Rent – Turret Books
The Suspension of the Moon – Oversteps Books
A Small Wave for Your Form – Oversteps Books
Temporal Bones – Oversteps Books

Simon Williams

Acknowledgements

Humouring, To Peter Powell, First Anniversary, Arbor Low and *Morning Call* first appeared in *A Weight of Small Things*. *How Snow Comes* was included in the 52 Anthology, Nine Arches Press.

Previous publications

Unbroken – Poetry Nottingham Pamphlets
A Weight of Small Things – Lincolnshire & Humberside Arts
Quirks – Oversteps Books
He/She – Itinerant Press
A Place Where Odd Animals Stand – Oversteps Books
Spotting Capybaras in the Work of Marc Chagall – Indigo Dreams
Inti – Oversteps Books

CONTENTS

Susan Taylor

Simon Williams

The Weather House

Mother's tiny house had a sandpaper roof
with eaves like a cuckoo clock's,
painted the colour of Dairy Milk chocolate.
The little cuboid chimney
reeled out a snippet of string
in place of white smoke.

An inch-high couple were glued each side
of a plank the width of a lolly stick
and stood on guard at twin front doors.
The dame wore an ever-so-cleverly woven apron,
which changed with the weather
from pink to blue.

The gent wore painted whiskers, waistcoat
and stove pipe hat, like the original toff.
How did they know when the sun came out?
How did they know when it rained?
Their little round heads were made of wood,
hearts wooden, too, and fingers fixed onto hips.

Two midgets from old Bohemia,
I checked every day before school,
to see whether Master or Mistress was out.
They knew about clouds and plain sailing,
as well as storms –
such was their magic.

I wanted to know what each got up to
when hidden alone in the dark
dwelling inside.
If you see them,
ask what it is they are doing
about the weather.

- 5 -

Humouring

I eat clouds, said the madman.
Cumulus taste of peppermint,
stratus like thin slices of pressed chicken,
but best, I like the lemon-coated cirrus.

I have heard, like sleep-walkers,
it is dangerous to cross such men;
I suck the liquorice of nimbus,
I replied.

He stared at me and said
You think I'm mad,
but I know you never touched
the nightshade thundercloud.

The Rainmaker
Because this cloud is transferring its might into a glass – Peter Redgrove

Cloud crushes into your glass as if it would be flowers, as if it is seeking flowers, or to be a flower – a huge purple bloom of a storm, smelling of nectar of electricity. I should pick the rain the same way I follow your footsteps through wet grass – crestfallen in the downpour. Your feet are bare, my arms are bare, the glass is singing a pure music. Who will drink this collection of rainwater of yours? Who will sink it first – a man with his toes questioning the earth; the cool skin of it shedding, or a woman with her arms out, calling for water's silk?

Clouds are anemones, dark centres brooding. I focus on light in your glass and a ghost of motion, which is the storm. You drink down the cloud around me, while I watch water running in tongues through the air. The sky is filling with swifts and swallows. Their wings are the colour of thunder.

Black and Blue

The black is staying blue longer;
someone's got a surplus
of blue to dispose of.
If, as seems likely,
this situation continues all summer,
there's going to be a large stockpile
of black by autumn.
Ten to one they'll then
flood the market with it;
we'll have more black
than we'll know what to do with.
Daylight robbery, that's what it is.

Yin Yang

Yin does what darkness does,
she spreads into every cell.

Yang follows through,
as fire through kindling,
prow of kayak
splicing river.

Yin shimmers
as rainbow obsidian does,
to hold and enfold
the swirling nature of colour.

Yang is a peacock
shaking his tail into rainbows.

Yin is the dreamer
while Yang is dream.
Yang is the dreamer
when Yin is dream.

To Peter Powell

We tried five places
in the wind before this heath.
Just off the road,
we now hold tautly to the lines
as the kite climbs fast
and children in each passing car
look on.

Tied to the diamond by sight,
we stumble over tufts,
but always our moves
translate to sweeps and flutters
in this bright air.
There is a magic in the scant control of flight;
a witchery that never falls to earth.

Out of Hibernation

All the songbirds outside in new light are awake,
snapping their bright eyes open and singing
to bring on their nestlings.

But I am asleep, I say
and still in the hold of a good healing dream,
full of dancing and longing and ferny shadow.

All the creatures in my brain are awake,
snapping their yellow eyes open like celandines,
but I am asleep, I say

and was dreaming that it was a warm day;
such a thing, very close,
very warm.

All the poems in my head are awake,
snippety snapping like winged things,
like so many sheets to the wind,

driving the agitant flow in the top of my heart.
But I am asleep I say and dreaming a shady wood;
everything moistened by leaf life in the air

as it wraps its kindling arms around me,
so I shed all my clothes for no reason
but for the feeling of being free.

On the Sun Coming Out for the First Time in May

I knew it was you
being discreet behind cloud,
like a swimmer changing on a beach.
I knew it was the overalls
that swim around our planet
in a launderette washer,
but it's still good to glimpse
your sparkle from the back of the drum
… and since I've now set up
this convoluted metaphor,

it's good to feel the warmth
of your heater and to know
my skin will soon be dry.
Shame it's taken you so long
to spin and tumble into sight,
but I guess we have ourselves to blame.
Hands in pockets, we need
a few more 50ps for windmills
and solar panels to keep
things turning and come clean.

I Finally Inherit My Mother's Love of Thunder

Thunder makes a huge voice of a word,
as it moves the whole sky around in its mouth,
bringing July to birth in a smoky ocean of cloud.

Thunder is abandoning the valley,
as I clamber clumsily out of bed, to probe
its monstrous largesse, the best way I can.

Thunder, not really vanished, leaves
a soft hold on my breath and a thick warm trace
in my tenuous garden, dry, and crying for rain.

Thunder, come back, be loud right now,
for I want to explore what you've done to open
a birthright, unchannelled before in my heart.

First Anniversary

To leave her parents unaware,
we go for subterfuge.
An evening's promenade
we walk, up on the tufted hill
and over it, she says
Look we've found the sun again.

Where the corn is ripe
and just the spikes of thistles live,
we lie down in celebration.
Like a banner, vapour trails away the sun
and as the sky sinks red,
we share its passing hint as warmth.

After, as the young beasts stare,
we wave to all
and nobody responds.
A year complete,
we climb the fence and brambles;
each small thorn is blunted for tonight.

Because a Rainbow

This is because a rainbow
simply slipped into the sky,
while I practise gathering clouds,
the one Chi Kung move I remember.

Simply slipped into the sky
in a backdrop of clouds, theatrically set,
the one Chi Kung move I remember
sips this high flown arch of light.

In a backdrop of clouds, theatrically set,
plum nimbostratus under white cumulus
sips this high flown arch of light;
a span of the spectrum's every colour.

Plum nimbostratus under white cumulus
drift along the rainbow's shoulder.
A span of the spectrum's every colour,
this heavenly bridge begins to swing open.

Drift along the rainbow's shoulder,
I'm anchored to how the sky shakes me free.
This heavenly bridge begins to swing open.
I'm here to mimic sun and rain's union.

I'm anchored to how the sky shakes me free;
it makes my breath and takes it away.
I am here to mimic sun and rain's union,
to fly in the face of all convention.

It makes my breath and takes it away,
while I practise gathering clouds
to fly in the face of all convention;
this is because a rainbow.

Arbor Low

an ancient monument in the Peak District

Our skins of blue cagoule
swell like boils,
as the wind fingers
the seams and squeezes
easily under the ties.

The henge flattens its grass
like fur against the rain.
Numbed by centuries to the
stinging flagellation, it still
sticks its tongue at the clouds.

The latest in a long line
of trippers,
we walk its ditch, circle
and barrow;
try to picture it

as a clearing in a forest,
now the peat beneath us.
The cows, with sodden flies,
crop the Arbor's coat,
free-ranged over its age.

They stand in the juicy mud,
where they've worn it bald.
There have always been cows here,
but the Arbor was old
when the first were calves.

Weather Warning

The cock on the weathervane crows for his hen.
Be advised, says the man who announces the weather,
the wind will be blustering 8, 9 or 10.

It's a three-pronged attack over moorland and fen
with rain, hail and gales, which will give it some leather.
The cock on the weathervane crows for his hen.

*This is a red warning; we don't know quite when
the whole system will piece itself back together;
for the present, its storming force 8, 9 or 10.*

What the future holds is beyond our ken;
you might as well ask some seaweed or heather,
or the cock on the weathervane calling his hen.

When you catch blue sky over your patch again,
be thankful that somehow the sun doesn't dither,
even if the storm force is 8, 9 or 10.

Life goes on – is amazing! Just listen,
the sky is playing the roof like a zither.
The cock on the weathervane crows for his hen
and the wind is blustering 8, 9 or 10.

Mammatocumulus

That cloud's all covered in boobs!
Tits I tell you,
bazungas hanging free
from the base of that nimbus.

From my notes,
I see they often indicate
strong storms,
something tornadic.

I picture them
as the combined armies
of Hyppolyta's Amazons,
all bending forwards.

I'm aware they
actually resemble
testicles more closely,
but to say

That cloud's all covered in balls
would be weird,
even for a meteorologist.
Wouldn't it, lads?

Calling Snow (featuring *How Snow Comes*)

Find a little something made of silver –
best if it's a teaspoon with the hour
and minute of your birth recorded,
as well as the month and year,
holding the mystery of your arrival.
It helps if you were born in December, of course,
although other months should do fine.

This is the light
mint white
which holds down
February's first
burst of fern.

You know snow lives in the mountains all year,
away over East, West and South,
where we think of oasis and cloud forest,
high peaks are touched by sky with glitters.
Far at the ends of everything, poles apart,
the ocean clings to shining mantels;
ice caps to shield earth's face.

It arrives gentle
as a mother
with a duvet
of sky-wide
smoke.

But did your mother or father
ever commission a spoon for your birth;
one that an astrologer could peer into,
to establish who you are?
And if you did get such a gift, was it lost, somehow,
in the way your life careered ahead?
We were all born – that's the thing,
with a silver spoon, or not – no matter.

For the purposes of this poem,
nickel or steel will do.
We move on, not to move mountains,
to get to the spell for snow.

After dark
under Scoriton's
one street lamp
orange petals
fall.

We're impatient, all of us,
let's say we're in London or on the Cornish Coast,
either way, somewhere near the land's end,
where snow has been hard to come by.
We're assuming you can get some kind of teaspoon,
there's not many places don't have them
and it's easy enough to squirrel one away in a pocket,
if need be.

This is the light
mint white
which holds down
February's first
burst of fern.

Now all you need is a goose down pillow,
an old fashioned one, like the one your grandfather had.
If it carries stains of an odd winter sniffle or two,
all the better – snow likes a nose that's been running.
Put a clean white pillowcase on the pillow,
just a plain one, like your granny made for herself.

It arrives gentle
as a mother
with a duvet
of sky-wide
smoke.

Take this pillow to bed, lay your teaspoon under it,
the bowl of it facing upwards. Then sleep,
pouring your dreams into it – any dream will do,
but let yourself be woken at dawn,
with a carefree head, like the one you had as a baby –
hungers acute, but easily satisfied.
Go to the window and peep through the curtain.
Are there white doves grazing in the meadow,
snowdrops along the lane by the stream,
white heather in the garden?
Have you caught sight of white hair
in your own reflection,
white ash in the grate, milk in the jug?
These are traces of the snow you forgot;
snow angels you made in your dreaming.

After dark
under Scoriton's
one street lamp
orange petals
fall.

Snow and Eyes

These days
there's insufficient cold
in all your valleys,
so you come up here
to make us.

Our lifespans are short,
but our race will last
as long as yours.

Beside Holwell Tor,
you make us in your image,
round and fat
with blindside grins
and stones for eyes.

We all look to the road,
where you disappear
as the sun drops.

snowdoll

on your path
i am foundling
smaller than human
when it is
full-term new-born

innocent
as he or she
and crystalline
the colour
of chased sky

one warm
as you
but smaller
thought me up
and pretty soon

someone
a similar size
will run up to take
my crisp round head
as a snowball

Digging In

At the outbreak of December,
he stoked the fire up, got in the fuel,
later, set dried flowers as best he could remember,
pulled up his chair, fed in a log for Yule.

While through the window, ice made jewels
on the willow, fixed like static tears,
he baked a loaf, sliced before it cooled
and toasted on the poker, to wassail New Year's

seeded hope. He drank a summer-coloured beer
and read the history of a badger sanctuary,
first-footed only when the aconites appeared
at the skirmished end of January.

Deli Morning

It's a Tuesday morning teeming with umbrellas,
the street outside more wet than high
and the daintiest of these umbrellas
come into Thrive Café to fold themselves
as flowers will, when rain rains hundreds and thousands.

A woodland spring picture, in here, works like a window
to where the bluebells on tables were picked.
The town trees outside, in newly furbished leaf,
are at one with this kind of downpour, driven to shake
their boughs in the gale and tender about them
their everyday multiplication of green.

Engrained

An English rose
and poured through it
all the rain in Kent.

Most of it on me,
a little for the land,
less for those with umbrellas.

It falls continuously.
I am slowly worn away;
eroded like the cliffs.

My sand is scattered
around soggy streets.
It collects in the gutters,

is mixed with other sand,
is swept away each night
to council sandpits.

Please watch where you tread;
there's a lot of me about.

Calling Rain

What is the largest entity moving over this land?
  It is the driven rain.
What do I see you walking into, my friend?
  It is the falling rain.
What wakes us from dreaming oblivion into yearning?
  It is the cool music of rain.
What is persistent, yet ever so gentle?
  It is a sparkle, alight in the rain.
What wears heads of granite to minute gems of mica?
  It is the macabre hammer of rain.
What grasps everything as energy dancing?
  It is the sweeping rain.
What enters our ears with hints of infinity?
  It is whispering tongues of rain.
What holds the imprint of all of our lives?
  It is a rhythm, a rift in the rain.
What rolls down into the river's eyes?
  the tears of the ocean, the rain.
What shears the edge off the wind,
  carves the land to its will,
    stops fire in its tracks?
    All of this,
      the incessant work of the rain.
What feeds all with its body,
    yet holds back, for us
      to bring in the harvest?
      This is the seasonal spirit
        in flight in wings of rain.
Where is the blueprint for rain,
      shape-shifting in cloud?

      Listen to a single drop
  hitting a china bowl on the windowsill,
          the bell it chimes.

Shipping Out

Under lowering cloud we're driving West;
this layered nimbus couldn't get much lower.
The only sunshine's over Lyonesse;

it seems to pace our Citroen's progress.
Travelling out of Devon for an hour,
under lowering cloud, we're driving West

for the third time in two weeks. No, I'm not stressed,
but feel the grey tarmac could devour
that glimpse of sunshine over Lyonesse.

It's holiday, no time to be depressed,
just let the sea and sand empower
us, ignore the cloud over the South West.

Visit galleries, seek the sun in well-expressed
bright oils; boats and terraces, the towers
of sunny, sunken Lyonesse.

Perhaps a boat trip out beyond Nanjizal's crest,
following that patch between the showers.
Under lowering cloud, we're shipping West.
The good stuff's far out over Lyonesse.

Spring Bank Holiday

Ignited,
day is a hot air balloon,
red on the horizon
rising:
freedom behind, freedom in front,
summer our bodies, summer our minds.

Now we are earthbound in soft locks of corn
and sun breaks may into flowers;
stamens push their pink
into the hard bright blue
that makes a sky.

Racing down roads of wild grass,
we reach beyond miles and wheels
into a great circus of sea,
where life runs open-lipped
over first stretches of sun,
bursting like the wallflowers
from water into wine.

Mist on the Dart

The river vaporises
as if it's making tea.

As we walk down
we test how it has filled.

It fits between the hedges
not our shoulders

covers like a Balaclava
not a cap

swirls like someone big
has danced Young Collins through it.

At the bottom of the lane
greens and browns are greyed, graded.

We take each other's hand
for fear of Friesians, river trolls.

Brother

He wakes to the ebullience of birds,
takes me through his meadows cut of dew
to golden calves, new offspring of his herd.
Head rung with the circle of acreage,
he tends bull and cows in marsh-light.

White as winter, summer gathers.
A halo burns around a rising sun.

I see him in the thrall of morning;
we share blind magic
in a brand new cuckoo's voice.
A tree with the top mast broken
yaws from low spirals of mist.

I come each time from further to come back here,
led by the whispering light of Jack-a-Lantern.

Morning Call

Out of sight,
it tries to escape the air,
to catch its voice like rungs
on a ladder.

She hears
its song, slowly separated
from the singing daylight
and gazes

for its stop
that punctuates a cloud.
The morning, late and mobile,
circles her,

confirms
their long acquaintance.
For a quick moment, the lark
listens.

And Again

Praise these May moments
when trees dress delicately,
green as peridot.

I'll be the arbour
hung with cherry blossom,
nectar for your bees.

You shall be the spine
that supports this ecstasy;
sweet is the stamen.

My lust is for growth
run riot in every peak,
most of all yours.

Stepping out to me
over the blush of petals,
I pluck you again

and again.

Heaven's Eternal Weather Forecast

It will be cloudy,
mainly underfoot.

Many thanks to Hannah Kopacz at *Made with Love by Hannah* (http://madewithlovebyhannah.com) for permission to use *The Weather House* artwork.

Thanks, also, to many friends who have encouraged us along the way with this project and, particularly, to Charlotte Chance for her enthusiasm and support in the development of *The Weather House* show. Find Charlotte at Sheherezade's Secret Hide-Out (http://sheherezadessecrethide-out.blogspot.uk) and at The Soul Apothecary on Instagram.

The Weather House is also a poetry show, inspired by our ever-changing climate and spiced with poems on climates of the heart. For further details, see:
www.susantaylor.co.uk.

To book the show, email:
susan@farmhouse.ac or simon@farmhouse.ac

Indigo Dreams Publishing Ltd
24, Forest Houses
Cookworthy Moor
Halwill
Beaworthy
Devon
EX21 5UU
www.indigodreams.co.uk